In Praise of Shadows

IN PRAISE

Foreword by Charles Moore

Afterword by Thomas J. Harper

OF SHADOWS

Jun'ichirō Tanizaki

Translated by Thomas J. Harper
and Edward G. Seidensticker

CHARLES E. TUTTLE CO.: PUBLISHERS

Published by the Charles E. Tuttle Company, Inc.
of Rutland, Vermont and Tokyo, Japan
with editorial offices
at Suido 1-chome, 2-6, Bunkyo-ku, Tokyo, Japan
by arrangement with
Leete's Island Books, Inc., New Haven, Connecticut

First Tuttle edition, 1984
Second printing, 1988

This essay has been made available
to Leete's Island Books with the gracious permission
of Mrs. Jun'ichirō Tanizaki.

This translation has received an award from the
Translation Center at Columbia University, made possible
by a grant from the National Endowment for the Arts.

ISBN 4-8053-0488-X
PRINTED IN JAPAN

FOREWORD

One of the basic human requirements is the need to dwell, and one of the central human acts is the act of inhabiting, of connecting ourselves, however temporarily, with a place on the planet which belongs to us, and to which we belong. This is not, especially in the tumultuous present, an easy act (as is attested by the uninhabited and uninhabitable no-places in cities everywhere), and it requires help: we need allies in inhabitation.

Fortunately, we have at hand many allies, if only we call on them; other upright objects, from towers to chimneys to columns, stand in for us in sympathetic imitation of our own upright stance. Flowers and gardens serve as testimonials to our own care, and breezes loosely captured can connect us with the very edge of the infinite. But in the West our most powerful ally is light. "The sun never knew how wonderful it was," the architect Louis Kahn said, "until it fell on the wall of a building." And for us the act of inhabitation is mostly performed in cahoots with the sun, our staunchest ally, bathing our world or flickering through it, helping give it light.

It comes with the thrill of a slap for us then to hear praise of shadows and darkness; so it is when there comes to us the excitement of realizing that musicians everywhere make their sounds to capture silence or that architects develop complex shapes just to envelop empty space. Thus darkness illuminates for us a culture very different from our own; but at the same time it helps us to look deep into ourselves to our own inhabitation of our world, as it describes with spine-tingling insights the traditional Japanese inhabitation of theirs. It could change our lives.

Charles Moore
School of Architecture, UCLA

In Praise of Shadows

What incredible pains the fancier of traditional architecture must take when he sets out to build a house in pure Japanese style, striving somehow to make electric wires, gas pipes, and water lines harmonize with the austerity of Japanese rooms—even someone who has never built a house for himself must sense this when he visits a teahouse, a restaurant, or an inn. For the solitary eccentric it is another matter, he can ignore the blessings of scientific civilization and retreat to some forsaken corner of the countryside; but a man who has a family and lives in the city cannot turn his back on the necessities of modern life—heating, electric lights, sanitary facilities—merely for the sake of doing things the Japanese way. The purist may rack his brain over the placement of a single telephone, hiding it behind the staircase or in a corner of the hallway, wherever he thinks it will least offend the eye. He may bury the wires rather than hang them in the garden, hide the switches in a closet or cupboard, run the cords behind a folding screen. Yet for all his ingenuity, his efforts often impress us as nervous, fussy, excessively contrived. For so accustomed are we to electric lights that the sight of a naked bulb beneath an ordinary milk glass shade seems simpler and more natural than any gratuitous attempt to hide it. Seen at dusk as one gazes out upon the countryside from the window of a train, the lonely light of a bulb under an old-fashioned shade, shining dimly from behind the white paper shoji of a thatch-roofed farmhouse, can seem positively elegant.

But the snarl and the bulk of an electric fan remain a bit out of place in a Japanese room. The ordinary householder, if he dislikes electric fans, can simply do without them. But if the family business involves the entertainment of customers in summertime, the gentleman of the house cannot afford to indulge his

1

own tastes at the expense of others. A friend of mine, the proprietor of a Chinese restaurant called the Kairakuen, is a thoroughgoing purist in matters architectural. He deplores electric fans and long refused to have them in his restaurant, but the complaints from customers with which he was faced every summer ultimately forced him to give in.

I myself have had similar experiences. A few years ago I spent a great deal more money than I could afford to build a house. I fussed over every last fitting and fixture, and in every case encountered difficulty. There was the shoji: for aesthetic reasons I did not want to use glass, and yet paper alone would have posed problems of illumination and security. Much against my will, I decided to cover the inside with paper and the outside with glass. This required a double frame, thus raising the cost. Yet having gone to all this trouble, the effect was far from pleasing. The outside remained no more than a glass door; while within, the mellow softness of the paper was destroyed by the glass that lay behind it. At that point I was sorry I had not just settled for glass to begin with. Yet laugh though we may when the house is someone else's, we ourselves accept defeat only after having a try at such schemes.

Then there was the problem of lighting. In recent years several fixtures designed for Japanese houses have come on the market, fixtures patterned after old floor lamps, ceiling lights, candle stands, and the like. But I simply do not care for them, and instead searched in curio shops for old lamps, which I fitted with electric light bulbs.

What most taxed my ingenuity was the heating system. No stove worthy of the name will ever look right in a Japanese room. Gas stoves burn with a terrific roar, and unless provided with a chimney, quickly bring headaches. Electric stoves, though at least free from these defects, are every bit as ugly as the rest. One solution would be to outfit the cupboards with heaters of the sort used in streetcars. Yet without the red glow of the coals, the whole mood of winter is lost and with it the pleasure of family gatherings round the fire. The best plan I could devise was to build a large sunken hearth, as in an old farmhouse. In this I installed an electric brazier, which worked well both for boiling tea water and for heating the room. Expensive it was, but at least so far as looks were concerned I counted it one of my successes.

Having done passably well with the heating system, I was then faced with the problem of bath and toilet. My Kairakuen friend could not bear to tile the tub and bathing area, and so built his guest bath entirely of wood. Tile, of course, is infinitely more practical and economical. But when ceiling, pillars, and paneling are of fine Japanese stock, the beauty of the room is utterly destroyed when the rest is done in sparkling tile. The effect may not seem so very displeasing while everything is still new, but as the years pass, and the beauty of the grain begins to emerge on the planks and pillars, that glittering expanse of white tile comes to seem as incongruous as the proverbial bamboo grafted to wood. Still, in the bath utility can to some extent be sacrificed to good taste. In the toilet somewhat more vexatious problems arise.

Every time I am shown to an old, dimly lit, and, I would add, impeccably clean toilet in a Nara or Kyoto temple, I am impressed with the singular virtues of Japanese architecture. The parlor may have its charms, but the Japanese toilet truly is a place of spiritual repose. It always stands apart from the main building, at the end of a corridor, in a grove fragrant with leaves and moss. No words can describe that sensation as one sits in the dim light, basking in the faint glow reflected from the shoji, lost in meditation or gazing out at the garden. The novelist Natsume Sōseki counted his morning trips to the toilet a great pleasure, "a physiological delight" he called it. And surely there could be no better place to savor this pleasure than a Japanese toilet where, surrounded by tranquil walls and finely grained wood, one looks out upon blue skies and green leaves.

As I have said there are certain prerequisites: a degree of dimness, absolute cleanliness, and quiet so complete one can hear the hum of a mosquito. I love to listen from such a toilet to the sound of softly falling rain, especially if it is a toilet of the Kantō region, with its long, narrow windows at floor level; there one can listen with such a sense of intimacy to the raindrops falling from the eaves and the trees, seeping into the earth as they wash over the base of a stone lantern and freshen the moss about the stepping stones. And the toilet is the perfect place to listen to the chirping of insects or the song of the birds, to view the moon, or to enjoy any of those poignant moments that mark the change of the seasons. Here, I suspect, is where haiku poets over the ages have come by a great many of their ideas. Indeed one could with some justice claim that of all the elements of Japanese architecture, the toilet is the most aesthetic. Our forebears, making poetry of everything in their lives, transformed what by rights should be the most unsanitary room in the house into a place of unsurpassed elegance, replete with fond associations with the beauties of nature. Compared to Westerners, who regard the toilet as utterly unclean and avoid even the mention of it in polite conversation, we are far more sensible and certainly in better taste. The Japanese toilet is, I must admit, a bit inconvenient to get to in the middle of the night, set apart from the main building as it is; and in winter there is always a danger that one might catch cold. But as the poet Saitō Ryokū has said, "elegance is frigid." Better that the place be as chilly as the out-of-doors; the steamy heat of a Western-style toilet in a hotel is most unpleasant.

Anyone with a taste for traditional architecture must agree that the Japanese toilet is perfection. Yet whatever its virtues in a place like a temple, where the dwelling is large, the inhabitants few, and everyone helps with the cleaning, in an ordinary household it is no easy task to keep it clean. No matter how fastidious one may be or how diligently one may scrub, dirt will show, particularly on a floor of wood or tatami matting. And so here too it turns out to be more hygienic and efficient to install modern sanitary facilities—tile and a flush toilet—though at the price of destroying all affinity with "good taste" and the "beauties of nature." That burst of light from those four white walls hardly puts one in a mood to relish Sōseki's "physiological delight." There is no denying the cleanliness; every nook and corner is pure white. Yet what need is there to remind us so forcefully of the issue of our own bodies. A beautiful woman, no matter how lovely her skin, would be considered indecent were she to show her bare buttocks or feet in the presence of others; and how very crude and tasteless to expose the toilet to such excessive illumination. The cleanliness of what can be seen only calls up the more clearly thoughts of what cannot be seen. In such places the distinction between the clean and the unclean is best left obscure, shrouded in a dusky haze.

Though I did install modern sanitary facilities when I built my own house, I at least avoided tiles, and had the floor done in camphor wood. To that extent I tried to create a Japanese atmosphere—but was frustrated

5

finally by the toilet fixtures themselves. As everyone knows, flush toilets are made of pure white porcelain and have handles of sparkling metal. Were I able to have things my own way, I would much prefer fixtures—both men's and women's—made of wood. Wood finished in glistening black lacquer is the very best; but even unfinished wood, as it darkens and the grain grows more subtle with the years, acquires an inexplicable power to calm and sooth. The ultimate, of course, is a wooden "morning glory" urinal filled with boughs of cedar; this is a delight to look at and allows not the slightest sound. I could not afford to indulge in such extravagances. I hoped I might at least have the external fittings made to suit my own taste, and then adapt these to a standard flushing mechanism. But the custom labor would have cost so much that I had no choice but to abandon the idea. It was not that I objected to the conveniences of modern civilization, whether electric lights or heating or toilets, but I did wonder at the time why they could not be designed with a bit more consideration for our own habits and tastes.

The recent vogue for electric lamps in the style of the old standing lanterns comes, I think, from a new awareness of the softness and warmth of paper, qualities which for a time we had forgotten; it stands as evidence of our recognition that this material is far better suited than glass to the Japanese house. But no toilet fixtures or stoves that are at all tasteful have yet come on the market. A heating system like my own, an electric brazier in a sunken hearth, seems to me ideal; yet no one ventures to produce even so simple a device as this (there are, of course, those feeble electric hibachi, but they provide no more heat than an ordinary charcoal hibachi); all that can be had ready-made are those ugly Western stoves.

There are those who hold that to quibble over matters of taste in the basic necessities of life is an extravagance, that as long as a house keeps out the cold and as long as food keeps off starvation, it matters little what they look like. And indeed for even the sternest ascetic the fact remains that a snowy day is cold, and there is no denying the impulse to accept the services of a heater if it happens to be there in front of one, no matter how cruelly its inelegance may shatter the spell of the day. But it is on occasions like this that I always think how different everything would be if we in the Orient had developed our own science. Suppose for instance that we had developed our own physics and chemistry: would not the techniques and industries based on them have taken a different form, would not our myriads of everyday gadgets, our medicines, the products of our industrial art—would they not have suited our national temper better than they do? In fact our conception of physics itself, and even the principles of chemistry, would probably differ from that of Westerners; and the facts we are now taught concerning the nature and function of light, electricity, and atoms might well have presented themselves in different form.

Of course I am only indulging in idle speculation; of scientific matters I know nothing. But had we devised independently at least the more practical sorts of inventions, this could not but have had profound influence upon the conduct of our everyday lives, and even upon government, religion, art, and business. The Orient quite conceivably could have opened up a world of technology entirely its own.

To take a trivial example near at hand: I wrote a magazine article recently comparing the writing brush with the fountain pen, and in the course of it I remarked that if the device had been invented by the ancient Chinese or Japanese it would surely have had a tufted end like our writing brush. The ink would not have been this bluish color but rather black, something like India ink, and it would have been made to seep down from the handle into the brush. And since we would have then found it inconvenient to write on Western paper, something near Japanese paper—even under mass production, if you will—would have been most in demand. Foreign ink and pen would not be as popular as they are; the talk of discarding our system of writing for Roman letters would be less noisy; people would still feel an affection for the old system. But more than that: our thought and our literature might not be imitating the West as they are, but might have pushed forward into new regions quite on their own. An insignificant little piece of writing equipment, when one thinks of it, has had a vast, almost boundless, influence on our culture.

But I know as well as anyone that these are the empty dreams of a novelist, and that having come this far we cannot turn back. I know that I am only grumbling to myself and demanding the impossible. If my complaints are taken for what they are, however, there can be no harm in considering how unlucky we have been, what losses we have suffered, in comparison with the Westerner. The Westerner has been able to move forward in ordered steps, while we have met superior civilization and have had to surrender to it, and we have had to leave a road we have followed for thousands of years. The missteps and inconveniences this has caused have, I think, been many. If we had been left alone we might not be much further now in a material way than we were five hundred years ago. Even now in the Indian and Chinese countryside life no doubt goes on much as it did when Buddha and Confucius were alive. But we would have gone only in a direction that suited us. We would have gone ahead very slowly, and yet it is not impossible that we would one day have discovered our own substitute for the trolley, the radio, the airplane of today. They would have been no borrowed gadgets, they would have been the tools of our own culture, suited to us.

One need only compare American, French, and German films to see how greatly nuances of shading and coloration can vary in motion pictures. In the photographic image itself, to say nothing of the acting and the script, there somehow emerge differences in national character. If this is true even when identical equipment, chemicals, and film are used, how much better our own photographic technology might have suited our complexion, our facial features, our climate, our land. And had we invented the phonograph and the radio, how much more faithfully they would reproduce the special character of our voices and our music. Japanese music is above all a music of reticence, of atmosphere. When recorded, or amplified by a loudspeaker, the greater part of its charm is lost. In conversation, too, we prefer the soft voice, the understatement. Most important of all are the pauses. Yet the phonograph and radio render these moments of silence utterly lifeless. And so we distort the arts themselves to curry favor for them with the machines. These machines are the inventions of Westerners, and are, as we might expect, well suited to the Western arts. But precisely on this account they put our own arts at a great disadvantage.

Paper, I understand, was invented by the Chinese, but Western paper is to us no more than something to be used, while the texture of Chinese paper and Japanese paper gives us a certain feeling of warmth, of calm and repose. Even the same white could as well be

9

one color for Western paper and another for our own. Western paper turns away the light, while our paper seems to take it in, to envelop it gently, like the soft surface of a first snowfall. It gives off no sound when it is crumpled or folded, it is quiet and pliant to the touch as the leaf of a tree.

As a general matter we find it hard to be really at home with things that shine and glitter. The Westerner uses silver and steel and nickel tableware, and polishes it to a fine brilliance, but we object to the practice. While we do sometimes indeed use silver for teakettles, decanters, or saké cups, we prefer not to polish it. On the contrary, we begin to enjoy it only when the luster has worn off, when it has begun to take on a dark, smoky patina. Almost every householder has had to scold an insensitive maid who has polished away the tarnish so patiently waited for.

Chinese food is now most often served on tableware made of tin, a material the Chinese could only admire for the patina it acquires. When new it resembles aluminum and is not particularly attractive; only after long use brings some of the elegance of age is it at all acceptable. Then, as the surface darkens, the line of verse etched upon it gives a final touch of perfection. In the hands of the Chinese this flimsy, glittering metal takes on a profound and somber dignity akin to that of their red unglazed pottery.

The Chinese also love jade. That strange lump of stone with its faintly muddy light, like the crystallized air of the centuries, melting dimly, dully back, deeper and deeper—are not we Orientals the only ones who know its charms? We cannot say ourselves what it is that we find in this stone. It quite lacks the brightness of a ruby or an emerald or the glitter of a diamond. But this much we can say: when we see that shadowy surface, we think how Chinese it is, we seem to find in its cloudiness the accumulation of the long Chinese past, we think how appropriate it is that the Chinese should admire that surface and that shadow.

It is the same with crystals. Crystals have recently been imported in large quantities from Chile, but Chilean crystals are too bright, too clear. We have long had crystals of our own, their clearness always moderated, made graver by a certain cloudiness. Indeed, we much prefer the "impure" varieties of crystal with opaque veins crossing their depths. Even of glass this is true; for is not fine Chinese glass closer to jade or agate than to Western glass? Glassmaking has long been known in the Orient, but the craft never developed as in the West. Great progress has been made, however, in the manufacture of pottery. Surely this has something to do with our national character. We do not dislike everything that shines, but we do prefer a pensive luster to a shallow brilliance, a murky light that, whether in a stone or an artifact, bespeaks a sheen of antiquity.

Of course this "sheen of antiquity" of which we hear so much is in fact the glow of grime. In both Chinese and Japanese the words denoting this glow describe a polish that comes of being touched over and over again, a sheen produced by the oils that naturally permeate an object over long years of handling—which is to say grime. If indeed "elegance is frigid," it can as well be described as filthy. There is no denying, at any rate, that among the elements of the elegance in which we take such delight is a measure of the unclean, the unsanitary. I suppose I shall sound terribly defensive if I say that Westerners attempt to expose every speck of grime and eradicate it, while we Orientals carefully preserve and even idealize it. Yet for better or for worse we do love things that bear the marks of grime, soot, and weather, and we love the colors and the sheen that

11

call to mind the past that made them. Living in these old houses among these old objects is in some mysterious way a source of peace and repose.

I have always thought that hospitals, those for the Japanese at any rate, need not be so sparkling white, that the walls, uniforms, and equipment might better be done in softer, more muted colors. Certainly the patients would be more reposed where they are able to lie on tatami matting surrounded by the sand-colored walls of a Japanese room. One reason we hate to go to the dentist is the scream of his drill; but the excessive glitter of glass and metal is equally intimidating. At a time when I was suffering from a severe nervous disorder, a dentist was recommended to me as having just returned from America with the latest equipment, but these tidings only made my hair stand on end. I chose instead to go to an old-fashioned dentist who maintained an office in an old Japanese house, a dentist of the sort found in small country towns. Antiquated medical equipment does have its drawbacks; but had modern medicine been developed in Japan we probably would have devised facilities and equipment for the treatment of the sick that would somehow harmonize with Japanese architecture. Here again we have to come off the loser for having borrowed.

There is a famous restaurant in Kyoto, the Waranjiya, one of the attractions of which was until recently that the dining rooms were lit by candlelight rather than electricity; but when I went there this spring after a long absence, the candles had been replaced by electric lamps in the style of old lanterns. I asked when this had happened, and was told that the change had taken place last year; several of their customers had complained that candlelight was too dim, and so they had been left no choice—but if I preferred the old way they should be happy to bring me a candlestand. Since that was what I had come for, I asked them to do so. And I realized then that only in dim half-light is the true beauty of Japanese lacquerware revealed. The rooms at the Waranjiya are about nine feet square, the size of a comfortable little tearoom, and the alcove pillars and ceilings glow with a faint smoky luster, dark even in the light of the lamp. But in the still dimmer light of the candlestand, as I gazed at the trays and bowls standing in the shadows cast by that flickering point of flame, I discovered in the gloss of this lacquerware a depth and richness like that of a still, dark pond, a beauty I had not before seen. It had not been mere chance, I realized, that our ancestors, having discovered lacquer, had conceived such a fondness for objects finished in it.

An Indian friend once told me that in his country ceramic tableware is still looked down upon, and that lacquerware is in far wider use. We, however, use ceramics for practically everything but trays and soup bowls; lacquerware, except in the tea ceremony and on formal occasions, is considered vulgar and inelegant. This, I suspect, is in part the fault of the much-vaunted "brilliance" of modern electric lighting. Darkness is an indispensible element of the beauty of lacquerware. Nowadays they make even a white lacquer, but the lacquerware of the past was finished in black, brown, or red, colors built up of countless layers of darkness, the inevitable product of the darkness in which life was lived. Sometimes a superb piece of black lacquerware, decorated perhaps with flecks of silver and gold—a box or a desk or a set of shelves—will seem to me unsettlingly garish and altogether vulgar. But render pitch black the void in which they stand, and light them not with the rays of the sun or electricity but rather a single lantern or candle: suddenly those garish objects turn somber, refined, dignified. Artisans of old, when they finished their works in lacquer and decorated them in sparkling patterns, must surely have had in mind dark rooms and sought to turn to good effect what feeble light there was. Their extravagant use of gold, too, I should imagine, came of understanding how it gleams forth from out of the darkness and reflects the lamplight.

Lacquerware decorated in gold is not something to be seen in a brilliant light, to be taken in at a single glance; it should be left in the dark, a part here and a part there picked up by a faint light. Its florid patterns recede into the darkness, conjuring in their stead an inexpressible aura of depth and mystery, of overtones but partly suggested. The sheen of the lacquer, set out in the night, reflects the wavering candlelight, announcing the drafts that find their way from time to time into the quiet room, luring one into a state of reverie. If the lacquer is taken away, much of the spell disappears from the dream world built by that strange light of candle and lamp, that wavering light beating the pulse of the night. Indeed the thin, impalpable, faltering light, picked up as though little rivers were running through the room, collecting little pools here and there, lacquers a pattern on the surface of the night itself.

Ceramics are by no means inadequate as tableware, but they lack the shadows, the depth of lacquerware. Ceramics are heavy and cold to the touch; they clatter and clink, and being efficient conductors of heat are not the best containers for hot foods. But lacquerware is light and soft to the touch, and gives off hardly a sound. I know few greater pleasures than holding a lacquer soup bowl in my hands, feeling upon my palms the weight of the liquid and its mild warmth. The sensation is something like that of holding a plump newborn baby. There are good reasons why lacquer soup bowls are still used, qualities which ceramic bowls simply do not possess. Remove the lid from a ceramic bowl, and there lies the soup, every nuance of its substance and color revealed. With lacquerware there is a beauty in that moment between removing the lid and lifting the bowl to the mouth when one gazes at the still, silent liquid in the dark depths of the bowl, its color hardly differing from that of the bowl itself. What lies within the darkness one cannot distinguish, but the palm senses the gentle movements of the liquid, vapor rises from within forming droplets on the rim, and the fragrance carried upon the vapor brings a delicate anticipation. What a world of difference there is between this moment and the moment when soup is served Western style, in a pale, shallow bowl. A moment of mystery, it might almost be called, a moment of trance.

Whenever I sit with a bowl of soup before me, listening to the murmur that penetrates like the far-off shrill of an insect, lost in contemplation of flavors to come, I feel as if I were being drawn into a trance. The experience must be something like that of the tea master who, at the sound of the kettle, is taken from himself as if upon the sigh of the wind in the legendary pines of Onoe.

It has been said of Japanese food that it is a cuisine to be looked at rather than eaten. I would go further and say that it is to be meditated upon, a kind of silent music evoked by the combination of lacquerware and the light of a candle flickering in the dark. Natsume Sōseki, in *Pillow of Grass*, praises the color of the confection yōkan; and is it not indeed a color to call forth meditation? The cloudy translucence, like that of jade; the faint, dreamlike glow that suffuses it, as if it had drunk into its very depths the light of the sun; the complexity and profundity of the color—nothing of the sort is to be found in Western candies. How simple and insignificant cream-filled chocolates seem by comparison. And when yōkan is served in a lacquer dish within whose dark recesses its color is scarcely distinguishable, then it is most certainly an object for meditation. You take its cool, smooth substance into your mouth, and it is as if the very darkness of the room were melting on your tongue; even undistinguished yōkan can then take on a mysteriously intriguing flavor.

In the cuisine of any country efforts no doubt are made to have the food harmonize with the tableware and the walls; but with Japanese food, a brightly lighted room and shining tableware cut the appetite in half. The dark miso soup that we eat every morning is one dish from the dimly lit houses of the past. I was once invited to a tea ceremony where miso was served; and when I saw the muddy, claylike color, quiet in a black lacquer bowl beneath the faint light of a candle, this soup that I usually take without a second thought seemed somehow to acquire a real depth, and to become infinitely more appetizing as well. Much the same may be said of soy sauce. In the Kyoto-Osaka region a particularly thick variety of soy is served with raw fish, pickles, and greens; and how rich in shadows is the viscous sheen of the liquid, how beautifully it blends with the darkness. White foods too—white miso, bean curd, fish cake, the white meat of fish— lose much of their beauty in a bright room. And above all there is rice. A glistening black lacquer rice cask set off in a dark corner is both beautiful to behold and a powerful stimulus to the appetite. Then the lid is briskly lifted, and this pure white freshly boiled food, heaped in its black container, each and every grain gleaming like a pearl, sends forth billows of warm steam—here is a sight no Japanese can fail to be moved by. Our cooking depends upon shadows and is inseparable from darkness.

I possess no specialized knowledge of architecture, but I understand that in the Gothic cathedral of the West, the roof is thrust up and up so as to place its pinnacle as high in the heavens as possible—and that herein is thought to lie its special beauty. In the temples of Japan, on the other hand, a roof of heavy tiles is first laid out, and in the deep, spacious shadows created by the eaves the rest of the structure is built. Nor is this true only of temples; in the palaces of the nobility and the houses of the common people, what first strikes the eye is the massive roof of tile or thatch and the heavy darkness that hangs beneath the eaves. Even at midday cavernous darkness spreads over all beneath the roof's edge, making entryway, doors, walls, and pillars all but invisible. The grand temples of Kyoto—Chion'in, Honganji—and the farmhouses of the remote countryside are alike in this respect: like most buildings of the past their roofs give the impression of possessing far greater weight, height, and surface than all that stands beneath the eaves.

In making for ourselves a place to live, we first spread a parasol to throw a shadow on the earth, and in the pale light of the shadow we put together a house. There are of course roofs on Western houses too, but they are less to keep off the sun than to keep off the wind and the dew; even from without it is apparent that they are built to create as few shadows as possible and to expose the interior to as much light as possible. If the roof of a Japanese house is a parasol, the roof of a Western house is no more than a cap, with as small a visor as possible so as to allow the sunlight to pene-

17

trate directly beneath the eaves. There are no doubt all sorts of reasons—climate, building materials—for the deep Japanese eaves. The fact that we did not use glass, concrete, and bricks, for instance, made a low roof necessary to keep off the driving wind and rain. A light room would no doubt have been more convenient for us, too, than a dark room. The quality that we call beauty, however, must always grow from the realities of life, and our ancestors, forced to live in dark rooms, presently came to discover beauty in shadows, ultimately to guide shadows towards beauty's ends.

And so it has come to be that the beauty of a Japanese room depends on a variation of shadows, heavy shadows against light shadows—it has nothing else. Westerners are amazed at the simplicity of Japanese rooms, perceiving in them no more than ashen walls bereft of ornament. Their reaction is understandable, but it betrays a failure to comprehend the mystery of shadows. Out beyond the sitting room, which the rays of the sun can at best but barely reach, we extend the eaves or build on a veranda, putting the sunlight at still greater a remove. The light from the garden steals in but dimly through paper-paneled doors, and it is precisely this indirect light that makes for us the charm of a room. We do our walls in neutral colors so that the sad, fragile, dying rays can sink into absolute repose. The storehouse, kitchen, hallways, and such may have a glossy finish, but the walls of the sitting room will almost always be of clay textured with fine sand. A luster here would destroy the soft fragile beauty of the feeble light. We delight in the mere sight of the delicate glow of fading rays clinging to the surface of a dusky wall, there to live out what little life remains to them. We never tire of the sight, for to us this pale glow and these dim shadows far surpass any ornament. And so, as we must if we are not to disturb the glow, we finish the walls with sand in a single neutral color. The hue may differ from room to room, but the degree of difference will be ever so slight; not so much a difference in color as in shade, a difference that will seem to exist only in the mood of the viewer. And from these delicate differences in the hue of the walls, the shadows in each room take on a tinge peculiarly their own.

Of course the Japanese room does have its picture alcove, and in it a hanging scroll and a flower arrangement. But the scroll and the flowers serve not as ornament but rather to give depth to the shadows. We value a scroll above all for the way it blends with the walls of the alcove, and thus we consider the mounting quite as important as the calligraphy or painting. Even the greatest masterpiece will lose its worth as a scroll if it fails to blend with the alcove, while a work of no particular distinction may blend beautifully with the room and set off to unexpected advantage both itself and its surroundings. Wherein lies the power of an otherwise ordinary work to produce such an effect? Most often the paper, the ink, the fabric of the mounting will possess a certain look of antiquity, and this look of antiquity will strike just the right balance with the darkness of the alcove and room.

We have all had the experience, on a visit to one of the great temples of Kyoto or Nara, of being shown a scroll, one of the temple's treasures, hanging in a large, deeply recessed alcove. So dark are these alcoves, even in bright daylight, that we can hardly discern the outlines of the work; all we can do is listen to the explanation of the guide, follow as best we can the all-but-invisible brush strokes, and tell ourselves how magnificent a painting it must be. Yet the combination of that blurred old painting and the dark alcove is one of absolute harmony. The lack of clarity, far from disturbing us, seems rather to suit the painting perfectly.

For the painting here is nothing more than another delicate surface upon which the faint, frail light can play; it performs precisely the same function as the sand-textured wall. This is why we attach such importance to age and patina. A new painting, even one done in ink monochrome or subtle pastels, can quite destroy the shadows of an alcove, unless it is selected with the greatest care.

A Japanese room might be likened to an inkwash painting, the paper-paneled shoji being the expanse where the ink is thinnest, and the alcove where it is darkest. Whenever I see the alcove of a tastefully built Japanese room, I marvel at our comprehension of the secrets of shadows, our sensitive use of shadow and light. For the beauty of the alcove is not the work of some clever device. An empty space is marked off with plain wood and plain walls, so that the light drawn into it forms dim shadows within emptiness. There is nothing more. And yet, when we gaze into the darkness that gathers behind the crossbeam, around the flower vase, beneath the shelves, though we know perfectly well it is mere shadow, we are overcome with the feeling that in this small corner of the atmosphere there reigns complete and utter silence; that here in the darkness immutable tranquility holds sway. The "mysterious Orient" of which Westerners speak probably refers to the uncanny silence of these dark places. And even we as children would feel an inexpressible chill as we peered into the depths of an alcove to which the sunlight had never penetrated. Where lies the key to this mystery? Ultimately it is the magic of shadows. Were the shadows to be banished from its corners, the alcove would in that instant revert to mere void.

This was the genius of our ancestors, that by cutting off the light from this empty space they imparted to the world of shadows that formed there a quality of mystery and depth superior to that of any wall painting or ornament. The technique seems simple, but was by no means so simply achieved. We can imagine with little difficulty what extraordinary pains were taken with each invisible detail—the placement of the window in the shelving recess, the depth of the crossbeam, the height of the threshold. But for me the most exquisite touch is the pale white glow of the shoji in the study bay; I need only pause before it and I forget the passage of time.

The study bay, as the name suggests, was originally a projecting window built to provide a place for reading. Over the years it came to be regarded as no more than a source of light for the alcove; but most often it serves not so much to illuminate the alcove as to soften the sidelong rays from without, to filter them through paper panels. There is a cold and desolate tinge to the light by the time it reaches these panels. The little sunlight from the garden that manages to make its way beneath the eaves and through the corridors has by then lost its power to illuminate, seems drained of the complexion of life. It can do no more than accentuate the whiteness of the paper. I sometimes linger before these panels and study the surface of the paper, bright, but giving no impression of brilliance.

In temple architecture the main room stands at a considerable distance from the garden; so dilute is the light there that no matter what the season, on fair days or cloudy, morning, midday, or evening, the pale, white glow scarcely varies. And the shadows at the interstices of the ribs seem strangely immobile, as if dust collected in the corners had become a part of the paper itself. I blink in uncertainty at this dreamlike luminescence, feeling as though some misty film were blunting my vision. The light from the pale white paper, powerless to dispel the heavy darkness of the alcove, is instead repelled by the darkness, creating a world of confusion where dark and light are indistinguishable. Have not you yourselves sensed a difference in the light that suffuses such a room, a rare tranquility not found in ordinary light? Have you never felt a sort of fear in the face of the ageless, a fear that in that room you might lose all consciousness of the passage of time, that untold years might pass and upon emerging you should find you had grown old and gray?

And surely you have seen, in the darkness of the innermost rooms of these huge buildings, to which sunlight never penetrates, how the gold leaf of a sliding door or screen will pick up a distant glimmer from the garden, then suddenly send forth an ethereal glow, a faint golden light cast into the enveloping darkness, like the glow upon the horizon at sunset. In no other setting is gold quite so exquisitely beautiful. You walk past, turning to look again, and yet again; and as you move away the golden surface of the paper glows ever more deeply, changing not in a flash, but growing slowly, steadily brighter, like color rising in the face of a giant. Or again you may find that the gold dust of the background, which until that moment had only a dull, sleepy luster, will, as you move past, suddenly gleam forth as if it had burst into flame.

How, in such a dark place, gold draws so much light to itself is a mystery to me. But I see why in ancient times statues of the Buddha were gilt with gold and why gold leaf covered the walls of the homes of the nobility. Modern man, in his well-lit house, knows nothing of the beauty of gold; but those who lived in the dark houses of the past were not merely captivated by its beauty, they also knew its practical value; for gold, in these dim rooms, must have served the function of a reflector. Their use of gold leaf and gold dust was not mere extravagance. Its reflective properties were put to use as a source of illumination. Silver and other metals quickly lose their gloss, but gold retains its brilliance indefinitely to light the darkness of the room. This is why gold was held in such incredibly high esteem.

I have said that lacquerware decorated in gold was made to be seen in the dark; and for this same reason were the fabrics of the past so lavishly woven of threads of silver and gold. The priest's surplice of gold brocade is perhaps the best example. In most of our city temples, catering to the masses as they do, the main hall will be brightly lit, and these garments of gold will seem merely gaudy. No matter how venerable a man the priest may be, his robes will convey no sense of his dignity. But when you attend a service at an old temple, conducted after the ancient ritual, you see how perfectly the gold harmonizes with the wrinkled skin of the old priest and the flickering light of the altar lamps, and how much it contributes to the solemnity of the occasion. As with lacquerware, the bold patterns remain for the most part hidden in darkness; only occasionally does a bit of gold or silver gleam forth.

I may be alone in thinking so, but to me it seems that nothing quite so becomes the Japanese skin as the costumes of the Nō theatre. Of course many are gaudy in the extreme, richly woven of gold and silver. But the Nō actor, unlike the Kabuki performer, wears no white powder. Whenever I attend the Nō I am impressed by the fact that on no other occasion is the beauty of the Japanese complexion set off to such advantage—the brownish skin with a flush of red that is so uniquely Japanese, the face like old ivory tinged with yellow. A robe woven or embroidered in patterns of gold or silver sets it off beautifully, as does a cloak of deep green or persimmon, or a kimono or divided skirt of a pure white, unpatterned material. And when the actor is a handsome young man with skin of fine texture and cheeks glowing with the freshness of youth, his good looks emerge as perfection, with a seductive charm quite different from a woman's. Here, one sees, is the beauty that made feudal lords lose themselves over their boy favorites.

Kabuki costumes, in the history plays and dance dramas, are no less colorful than Nō costumes; and Kabuki is commonly thought to have far greater sexual appeal than Nō. But to the adept the opposite is true. At first Kabuki will doubtless seem the more erotic and visually beautiful; but, whatever they may have been in the past, the gaudy Kabuki colors under the glare of the Western floodlamps verge on a vulgarity of which one quickly tires. And if this is true of the costumes it is all the more true of the makeup. Beautiful though such a face may be, it is after all made up; it has nothing of the immediate beauty of the flesh. The Nō actor performs with no makeup on his face or neck or hands. The man's beauty is his own; our eyes are in no way deceived. And so there is never that disappointment with the Nō actor that we feel upon seeing the unadorned face of the Kabuki actor who has played the part of a woman or handsome young man. Rather we are amazed how much the man's looks are enhanced by the gaudy costume of a medieval warrior—a man with skin like our own, in a costume we would not have thought would become him in the slightest.

I once saw Kongō Iwao play the Chinese beauty Yang Kuei-fei in the Nō play *Kōtei*, and I shall never forget the beauty of his hands showing ever so slightly from beneath his sleeves. As I watched his hands, I would occasionally glance down at my own hands resting on my knees. Again, and yet again, I looked back at the actor's hands, comparing them with my own; and there was no difference between them. Yet strangely the hands of the man on the stage were indescribably beautiful, while those on my knees were but ordinary hands. In the Nō only the merest fraction of the actor's flesh is visible—the face, the neck, the hands—and when a mask is worn, as for the role of Yang Kuei-fei, even the face is hidden; and so what little flesh can be seen creates a singularly strong impression. This was particularly true of Kongō Iwao; but even the hands of an ordinary actor—which is to say the hands of an average, undistinguished Japanese—have a remarkable erotic power which we would never notice were we to see the man in modern attire.

I would repeat that this is by no means true only of youthful or handsome actors. An ordinary man's lips will not ordinarily attract us; and yet on the Nō stage, the deep red glow and the moist sheen that come over them give a texture far more sensual than the painted lips of a woman. Chanting may keep the actor's lips constantly moist, but there is more to his beauty than this. Then again, the flush of red in the cheeks of a child actor can emerge with extraordinary freshness—an effect which in my experience is most striking against a costume in which green predominates. We might expect this to be true of a fair-skinned child; yet remarkably the reddish tinge shows to better effect on a dark-skinned child. For with the fair child the contrast between white and red is too marked, and the dark, somber colors of the Nō costume stand out too strongly, while against the brownish cheeks of the darker child the red is not so conspicuous, and costume and face complement each other beautifully. The perfect harmony of the yellow skin with garments of a subdued green or brown forces itself upon our attention as at no other time.

Were the Nō to be lit by modern floodlamps, like the Kabuki, this sense of beauty would vanish under the harsh glare. And thus the older the structure the better, for it is an essential condition of the Nō that the stage be left in the darkness in which it has stood since antiquity. A stage whose floor has acquired a natural gloss, whose beams and backdrop glow with a dark light, where the darkness beneath the rafters and eaves hangs above the actors' heads as if a huge temple bell were suspended over them—such is the proper place for Nō. Its recent ventures into huge auditoriums may have something to recommend them, but in such a setting the true beauty of the Nō is all but lost.

The darkness in which the Nō is shrouded and the beauty that emerges from it make a distinct world of shadows which today can be seen only on the stage; but in the past it could not have been far removed from daily life. The darkness of the Nō stage is after all the darkness of the domestic architecture of the day; and Nō costumes, even if a bit more splendid in pattern and color, are by and large those that were worn by court nobles and feudal lords. I find the thought fascinating: to imagine how very handsome, by comparison with us today, the Japanese of the past must have been in their resplendent dress—particularly the warriors of the fifteenth and sixteenth centuries. The Nō sets before us the beauty of Japanese manhood at its finest. What grand figures those warriors who traversed the battlefields of old must have cut in their full regalia emblazoned with family crests, the somber ground and gleaming embroidery setting off strong-boned faces burnished a deep bronze by wind and rain.

26

Every devotee of the Nō finds a certain portion of his pleasure in speculations of this sort; for the thought that the highly colored world on the stage once existed just as we see it imparts to the Nō a historical fascination quite apart from the drama.

But the Kabuki is ultimately a world of sham, having little to do with beauty in the natural state. It is inconceivable that the beautiful women of old—to say nothing of the men—bore any resemblance to those we see on the Kabuki stage. The women of the Nō, portrayed by masked actors, are far from realistic; but the Kabuki actor in the part of a woman inspires not the slightest sense of reality. The failure is the fault of excessive lighting. When there were no modern floodlamps, when the Kabuki stage was lit by the meager light of candles and lanterns, actors must have been somewhat more convincing in women's roles. People complain that Kabuki actors are no longer really feminine, but this is hardly the fault of their talents or looks. If actors of old had had to appear on the bright stage of today, they would doubtless have stood out with a certain masculine harshness, which in the past was discreetly hidden by darkness. This was brought home to me vividly when I saw the aging Baikō in the role of the young Okaru. A senseless and extravagant use of lights, I thought, has destroyed the beauty of Kabuki.

A knowledgeable Osaka gentleman has told me that the Bunraku puppet theatre was for long lit by lamplight, even after the introduction of electricity in the Meiji era, and that this method was far more richly suggestive than modern lighting. Even now I find the puppets infinitely more real than the actors of female Kabuki parts. But in the dim lamplight, the hard lines of the puppet features softened, the glistening white of

27

their faces muted—a chill comes over me when I think of the uncanny beauty the puppet theatre must once have had.

The female puppets consist only of a head and a pair of hands. The body, legs, and feet are concealed within a long kimono, and so the operators need only work their hands within the costume to suggest movements. To me this is the very epitome of reality, for a woman of the past did indeed exist only from the collar up and the sleeves out; the rest of her remained hidden in darkness. A woman of the middle or upper ranks of society seldom left her house, and when she did she shielded herself from the gaze of the public in the dark recesses of her palanquin. Most of her life was spent in the twilight of a single house, her body shrouded day and night in gloom, her face the only sign of her existence. Though the men dressed somewhat more colorfully than they do today, the women dressed more somberly. Daughters and wives of the merchant class wore astonishingly severe dress. Their clothing was in effect no more than a part of the darkness, the transition between darkness and face.

One thinks of the practice of blackening the teeth. Might it not have been an attempt to push everything except the face into the dark? Today this ideal of beauty has quite disappeared from everyday life, and one must go to an ancient Kyoto teahouse, such as the Sumiya in Shimabara, to find traces of it. But when I think back to my own youth in the old downtown section of Tokyo, and I see my mother at work on her sewing in the dim light from the garden, I think I can imagine a little what the old Japanese woman was like. In those days—it was around 1890—the Tokyo townsman still lived in a dusky house, and my mother, my aunts, my relatives, most women of their age, still blackened their teeth. I do not remember what they wore for everyday, but when they went out it was often in a gray kimono with a small, modest pattern.

My mother was remarkably slight, under five feet I should say, and I do not think that she was unusual for her time. I can put the matter strongly: women in those days had almost no flesh. I remember my mother's face and hands, I can clearly remember her feet, but I can remember nothing about her body. She reminds me of the statue of Kannon in the Chūgūji, whose body must be typical of most Japanese women of the past. The chest as flat as a board, breasts paper-thin, back, hips, and buttocks forming an undeviating straight line, the whole body so lean and gaunt as to seem out of proportion with the face, hands, and feet, so lacking in substance as to give the impression not of flesh but of a stick—must not the traditional Japanese woman have had just such a physique? A few are still about—the aged lady in an old-fashioned household, some few geisha. They remind me of stick dolls, for in fact they are nothing more than poles upon which to hang clothes. As with the dolls their substance is made up of layer upon layer of clothing, bereft of which only an ungainly pole remains. But in the past this was sufficient. For a woman who lived in the dark it was enough if she had a faint, white face—a full body was unnecessary.

I suppose it is hard for those who praise the fleshly beauty we see under today's bright lights to imagine the ghostly beauty of those older women. And there may be some who argue that if beauty has to hide its weak points in the dark it is not beauty at all. But we Orientals, as I have suggested before, create a kind of beauty of the shadows we have made in out-of-the-way places. There is an old song that says "the brushwood we gather—stack it together, it makes a hut; pull it apart, a field once more." Such is our way of thinking—we find beauty not in the thing itself but in the patterns of shadows, the light and the darkness, that one thing against another creates.

A phosphorescent jewel gives off its glow and color in the dark and loses its beauty in the light of day. Were it not for shadows, there would be no beauty. Our ancestors made of woman an object inseparable from darkness, like lacquerware decorated in gold or mother-of-pearl. They hid as much of her as they could in shadows, concealing her arms and legs in the folds of long sleeves and skirts, so that one part and one only stood out—her face. The curveless body may, by comparison with Western women, be ugly. But our thoughts do not travel to what we cannot see. The unseen for us does not exist. The person who insists upon seeing her ugliness, like the person who would shine a hundred-candlepower light upon the picture alcove, drives away whatever beauty may reside there.

Why should this propensity to seek beauty in darkness be so strong only in Orientals? The West too has known a time when there was no electricity, gas, or petroleum, and yet so far as I know the West has never been disposed to delight in shadows. Japanese ghosts have traditionally had no feet; Western ghosts have feet, but are transparent. As even this trifle suggests, pitch darkness has always occupied our fantasies, while in the West even ghosts are as clear as glass. This is true too of our household implements: we prefer colors compounded of darkness, they prefer the colors of sunlight. And of silver and copperware: we love them for the burnish and patina, which they consider unclean, unsanitary, and polish to a glittering brilliance. They paint their ceilings and walls in pale colors to drive out as many of the shadows as they can.

We fill our gardens with dense plantings, they spread out a flat expanse of grass.

But what produces such differences in taste? In my opinion it is this: we Orientals tend to seek our satisfactions in whatever surroundings we happen to find ourselves, to content ourselves with things as they are; and so darkness causes us no discontent, we resign ourselves to it as inevitable. If light is scarce then light is scarce; we will immerse ourselves in the darkness and there discover its own particular beauty. But the progressive Westerner is determined always to better his lot. From candle to oil lamp, oil lamp to gaslight, gaslight to electric light—his quest for a brighter light never ceases, he spares no pains to eradicate even the minutest shadow.

But beyond such differences in temperament, I should like to consider the importance of the difference in the color of our skin. From ancient times we have considered white skin more elegant, more beautiful than dark skin, and yet somehow this whiteness of ours differs from that of the white races. Taken individually there are Japanese who are whiter than Westerners and Westerners who are darker than Japanese, but their whiteness and darkness is not the same. Let me take an example from my own experience. When I lived on the Bluff in Yokohama I spent a good deal of my leisure in the company of foreign residents, at their banquets and balls. At close range I was not particularly struck by their whiteness, but from a distance I could distinguish them quite clearly from the Japanese. Among the Japanese were ladies who were dressed in gowns no less splendid than the foreigners', and whose skin was whiter than theirs. Yet from across the room these ladies, even one alone, would stand out unmistakably from amongst a group of foreigners. For the Japanese complexion, no matter how white, is tinged by a slight cloudiness. These women were in no way reticent about powdering themselves. Every bit of exposed flesh—even their backs and arms—they covered with a thick coat of white. Still they could not efface the darkness that lay below their skin. It was as plainly visible as dirt at the bottom of a pool of pure water. Between the fingers, around the nostrils, on the nape of the neck, along the spine—about these places especially, dark, almost dirty, shadows gathered. But the skin of the Westerners, even those of a darker complexion, had a limpid glow. Nowhere were they tainted by this gray shadow. From the tops of their heads to the tips of their fingers the whiteness was pure and unadulterated. Thus it is that when one of us goes among a group of Westerners it is like a grimy stain on a sheet of white paper. The sight offends even our own eyes and leaves none too pleasant a feeling.

We can appreciate, then, the psychology that in the past caused the white races to reject the colored races. A sensitive white person could not but be upset by the shadow that even one or two colored persons cast over a social gathering. What the situation is today I do not know, but at the time of the American Civil War, when persecution of Negroes was at its most intense, the hatred and scorn were directed not only at full-blooded Negroes, but at mulattos, the children of mulattos, and even the children of mulattos and whites. Those with the slightest taint of Negro blood, be it but a half, a quarter, a sixteenth, or a thirty-second, had to be ferreted out and made to suffer. Not even those who at a glance were indistinguishable from pure-blooded whites, but among whose ancestors two or three generations earlier there had been a Negro, escaped the searching gaze, no matter how faint the tinge that lay hidden beneath their white skin.

And so we see how profound is the relationship between shadows and the yellow races. Because no one likes to show himself to bad advantage, it is natural that we should have chosen cloudy colors for our food and clothing and houses, and sunk ourselves back into the shadows. I am not saying that our ancestors were conscious of the cloudiness in their skin. They cannot have known that a whiter race existed. But one must conclude that something in their sense of color led them naturally to this preference.

Our ancestors cut off the brightness on the land from above and created a world of shadows, and far in the depths of it they placed woman, marking her the whitest of beings. If whiteness was to be indispensible to supreme beauty, then for us there was no other way, nor do I find this objectionable. The white races are fair-haired, but our hair is dark; so nature taught us the laws of darkness, which we instinctively used to turn a yellow skin white. I have spoken of the practice of blackening the teeth, but was not the shaving of the eyebrows also a device to make the white face stand out? What fascinates me most of all, however, is that green, iridescent lipstick, so rarely used today even by Kyoto geisha. One can guess nothing of its power unless one imagines it in the low, unsteady light of a candle. The woman of old was made to hide the red of her mouth under green-black lipstick, to put shimmering ornaments in her hair; and so the last trace of color was taken from her rich skin. I know of nothing whiter than the face of a young girl in the wavering shadow of a lantern, her teeth now and then as she smiles shining a lacquered black through lips like elfin fires. It is whiter than the whitest white woman I can imagine. The whiteness of the white woman is clear, tangible, familiar, it is not this other-worldly whiteness. Perhaps the latter does not even exist. Perhaps it is only a mischievous trick of light and shadow, a thing of a moment only. But even so it is enough. We can ask for nothing more.

And while I am talking of this whiteness I want to talk also of the color of the darkness that enfolds it. I think of an unforgettable vision of darkness I once had when I took a friend from Tokyo to the old Sumiya teahouse in Kyoto. I was in a large room, the "Pine Room" I think, since destroyed by fire, and the darkness, broken only by a few candles, was of a richness quite different from the darkness of a small room. As we came in the door an elderly waitress with shaven eyebrows and blackened teeth was kneeling by a candle behind which stood a large screen. On the far side of the screen, at the edge of the little circle of light, the darkness seemed to fall from the ceiling, lofty, intense, monolithic, the fragile light of the candle unable to pierce its thickness, turned back as from a black wall. I wonder if my readers know the color of that "darkness seen by candlelight." It was different in quality from darkness on the road at night. It was a repletion, a pregnancy of tiny particles like fine ashes, each particle luminous as a rainbow. I blinked in spite of myself, as though to keep it out of my eyes.

Smaller rooms are the fashion now, and even if one were to use candles in them one would not get the color of that darkness; but in the old palace and the old house of pleasure the ceilings were high, the skirting corridors were wide, the rooms themselves were usually tens of feet long and wide, and the darkness must always have pressed in like a fog. The elegant aristocrat of old was immersed in this suspension of ashen particles, soaked in it, but the man of today, long used to the electric light, has forgotten that such a darkness existed. It must have been simple for specters to appear in a "visible darkness," where always something seemed to be flickering and shimmering, a darkness that on occasion held greater terrors than darkness out-of-doors. This was the darkness in which ghosts and monsters were active, and indeed was not the woman who lived in it, behind thick curtains, behind layer after layer of screens and doors—was she not of a kind with them? The darkness wrapped her round tenfold, twentyfold, it filled the collar, the sleeves of her kimono, the folds of her skirt, wherever a hollow invited. Further yet: might it not have been the reverse, might not the darkness have emerged from her mouth and those black teeth, from the black of her hair, like the thread from the great earth spider?

The novelist Takebayashi Musōan said when he returned from Paris a few years ago that Tokyo and Osaka were far more brightly lit than any European city; that even on the Champs Élysées there were still houses lit by oil lamps, while in Japan hardly a one remained unless in a remote mountain village. Perhaps no two countries in the world waste more electricity than America and Japan, he said, for Japan is only too anxious to imitate America in every way it can. That was some four or five years ago, before the vogue for neon signs. Imagine his surprise were he to come home today, when everything is so much brighter.

Yamamoto Sanehiko, president of the Kaizō publishing house, told me of something that happened when he escorted Dr. Einstein on a trip to Kyoto. As the train neared Ishiyama, Einstein looked out the window and remarked, "Now that is terribly wasteful." When asked what he meant, Einstein pointed to an electric lamp burning in broad daylight. "Einstein is a Jew, and so he is probably very careful about such things"—this was Yamamoto's interpretation. But the truth of the matter is that Japan wastes more electric light than any Western country except America.

This calls to mind another curious Ishiyama story. This year I had great trouble making up my mind where to go for the autumn moon-viewing. Finally, after much perplexed head-scratching, I decided on the Ishiyama Temple. The day before the full moon, however, I read in the paper that there would be loudspeakers in the woods at Ishiyama to regale the moon-viewing guests with phonograph records of the Moonlight Sonata. I canceled my plans immediately. Loudspeakers were bad enough, but if it could be assumed that they would set the tone, then there would surely be floodlights too strung all over the mountain. I remember another ruined moon-viewing, the year we took a boat on the night of the harvest full moon and sailed out over the lake of the Suma Temple. We put together a party, we had our refreshments in lacquered boxes, we set bravely out. But the margin of the lake was decorated brilliantly with electric lights in five colors. There was indeed a moon if one strained one's eyes for it.

So benumbed are we nowadays by electric lights that we have become utterly insensitive to the evils of excessive illumination. It does not matter all that much in the case of the moon, I suppose, but teahouses, restaurants, inns, and hotels are sure to be lit far too extravagantly. Some of this may be necessary to attract customers, but when the lights are turned on in summer even before dark it is a waste, and worse than the waste is the heat. I am upset by it wherever I go in the summer. Outside it will be cool, but inside it will be ridiculously hot, and more often than not because of lights too strong or too numerous. Turn some of them off and in no time at all the room is refreshingly cool.

Yet curiously neither the guests nor the owner seem to realize this. A room should be brighter in winter, but dimmer in summer; it is then appropriately cool, and does not attract insects. But people will light the lights, then switch on an electric fan to combat the heat. The very thought annoys me.

One can endure a Japanese room all the same, for ultimately the heat escapes through the walls. But in a Western-style hotel circulation is poor, and the floors, walls, and ceilings drink in the heat and throw it back from every direction with unbearable intensity. The worst example, alas, is the Miyako Hotel in Kyoto, as anyone who has been in its lobby on a summer's evening should agree. It stands on high ground, facing north, commanding a view of Mount Hiei, Nyoigatake, the Kurodani pagoda, the forests, the green hills of Higashiyama—a splendidly fresh and clean view, all the more disappointing for being so. Should a person of a summer's evening set out to refresh himself among purple hills and crystal streams, to take in the cool breeze that blows through the tower on the heights, he will only find himself beneath a white ceiling dotted with huge milk glass lights, each sending forth a blinding blaze.

As in most recent Western-style buildings, the ceilings are so low that one feels as if balls of fire were blazing directly above one's head. "Hot" is no word for the effect, and the closer to the ceiling the worse it is—your head and neck and spine feel as if they were being roasted. One of these balls of fire alone would suffice to light the place, yet three or four blaze down from the ceiling, and there are smaller versions on the walls and pillars, serving no function but to eradicate every trace of shadow. And so the room is devoid of shadows. Look about and all you will see are white walls, thick red pillars, a garish floor done in mosaic patterns looking much like a freshly printed lithograph—all oppressively hot. When you enter from the corridor the difference in temperature is all too apparent. No matter how cool a breeze blows in, it is instantly transformed to hot wind.

I have stayed at the Miyako several times and think fondly of it. My warnings are given with the friendliest of intentions. It is a pity that so lovely a view, so perfect a place for enjoying the cool of a summer's night, should be utterly destroyed by electric lights. The Japanese quite aside, I cannot believe that Westerners, however much they may prefer light, can be other than appalled at the heat, and I have no doubt they would see immediately the improvement in turning down the lights. The Miyako is by no means the only example. The Imperial Hotel, with its indirect lighting, is on the whole a pleasant place, but in summer even it might be a bit darker.

Light is used not for reading or writing or sewing but for dispelling the shadows in the farthest corners, and this runs against the basic idea of the Japanese room. Something is salvaged when a person turns off the lights at home to save money, but at inns and restaurants there is inevitably too much light in the halls, on the stairs, in the doorway, the gate, the garden. The rooms and the water and stones outside become flat and shallow. There are advantages for keeping warm in the winter, I suppose, but in the summer, no matter to what isolated mountain resort a person flees to escape the heat, he has a disappointment waiting if it is an inn or hotel he is going to. I have found myself that the best way to keep cool is to stay at home, open the doors, and stretch out in the dark under a mosquito net.

I recently read a newspaper or magazine article about the complaints of old women in England. When they were young, they said, they respected their elders and took good care of them; but their own daughters care nothing at all for them, and avoid them as though they were somehow dirty. The morals of the young, they lamented, are not what they once were. It struck me that old people everywhere have much the same complaints. The older we get the more we seem to think that everything was better in the past. Old people a century ago wanted to go back two centuries, and two centuries ago they wished it were three centuries earlier. Never has there been an age that people have been satisfied with. But in recent years the pace of progress has been so precipitous that conditions in our own country go somewhat beyond the ordinary. The changes that have taken place since the Restoration of 1867 must be at least as great as those of the preceding three and a half centuries.

It will seem odd, I suppose, that I should go on in this vein, as if I too were grumbling in my dotage. Yet of this I am convinced, that the conveniences of modern culture cater exclusively to youth, and that the times grow increasingly inconsiderate of old people. Let me take a familiar example: now that we cannot cross an intersection without consulting a traffic signal, old people can no longer venture confidently out into the streets. For someone sufficiently well-off to be driven about in an automobile there may be no problem, but on those rare occasions when I go into Osaka, it sets every nerve in my body on edge to cross from one side of the street to the other. If the signal is in the middle of the intersection it is easy enough to see it; but it is all but impossible to pick out a stop light that stands off to the side, where no one would ever expect to find it. If the intersection is broad, it is only too easy to confuse the light for facing traffic with the light for crossing traffic. It seemed to me the end of everything when the traffic policeman came to Kyoto.

Now one must travel to such small cities as Nishinomiya, Sakai, Wakayama, or Fukuyama for the feel of Japan.

The same is true of food. In a large city it takes a concerted search to turn up a dish that will be palatable to an old person. Not long ago a newspaper reporter came to interview me on the subject of unusual foods, and I described to him the persimmon-leaf sushi made by the people who live deep in the mountains of Yoshino—and which I shall take the opportunity to introduce to you here. To every ten parts of rice one part of saké is added just when the water comes to a boil. When the rice is done it should be cooled thoroughly, after which salt is applied to the hands and the rice molded into bite-size pieces. At this stage the hands must be absolutely free of moisture, the secret being that only salt should touch the rice. Thin slices of lightly salted salmon are placed on the rice, and each piece is wrapped in a persimmon leaf, the surface of the leaf facing inward. Both the persimmon leaves and the salmon should be wiped with a dry cloth to remove any moisture. Then in a rice tub or sushi box, the interior of which is perfectly dry, the pieces are packed standing on end so that no space remains between them, and the lid is put in place and weighted with a heavy stone, as in making pickles. Prepared in the evening, the sushi should be ready to eat the next morning. Though the taste is best on the first day, it remains edible for two or three days. A slight bit of vinegar is sprinkled over each piece with a sprig of bitter nettle just before eating.

I learned of the dish from a friend who had been to Yoshino and found it so exceptionally good that he took the trouble to learn how to make it—but if you have the persimmon leaves and salted salmon it can be made anywhere. You need only remember to keep out every trace of moisture, and to cool the rice completely. I made some myself, and it was very good indeed. The oil of the salmon and the slight hint of salt give just the proper touch of seasoning to the rice, and the salmon becomes as soft as if it were fresh—the flavor is indescribable, and far better than the sushi one gets in Tokyo. I have become so fond of it that I ate almost nothing else this summer. What impressed me, however, was that this superb method of preparing salted salmon was the invention of poor mountain people. Yet a sampling of the various regional cuisines suggests that in our day country people have far more discriminating palates than city people, and that in this respect they enjoy luxuries we cannot begin to imagine.

And so as time goes by, old people give up the cities and retire to the country; and yet there is not much cause for hope there either, for country towns are year by year going the way of Kyoto, their streets strung with bright lights. There are those who say that when civilization progresses a bit further transportation facilities will move into the skies and under the ground, and that our streets will again be quiet, but I know perfectly well that when that day comes some new device for torturing the old will be invented. "Out of our way, old people," we say, and they have no recourse but to shrink back into their houses, to make whatever tidbits they can for themselves, and to enjoy their evening saké as best they can to the accompaniment of the radio.

But do not think that old people are the only ones to find fault. The author of the "Vox Populi Vox Dei" column in the Osaka *Asahi* recently castigated city officials who quite needlessly cut a swath through a forest and leveled a hill in order to build a highway through Minō Park. I was somewhat encouraged; for to snatch away from us even the darkness beneath trees that stand deep in the forest is the most heartless of crimes. At this rate every place of any beauty in Nara or in the suburbs of Kyoto and Osaka, as the price of being turned over to the masses, will be denuded of trees. But again I am grumbling.

I am aware of and most grateful for the benefits of the age. No matter what complaints we may have, Japan has chosen to follow the West, and there is nothing for her to do but move bravely ahead and leave us old ones behind. But we must be resigned to the fact that as long as our skin is the color it is the loss we have suffered cannot be remedied. I have written all this because I have thought that there might still be somewhere, possibly in literature or the arts, where something could be saved. I would call back at least for literature this world of shadows we are losing. In the mansion called literature I would have the eaves deep and the walls dark, I would push back into the shadows the things that come forward too clearly, I would strip away the useless decoration. I do not ask that this be done everywhere, but perhaps we may be allowed at least one mansion where we can turn off the electric lights and see what it is like without them.

AFTERWORD

In Praise of Shadows is an essay on aesthetics by an eminent Japanese novelist; but to sum it up as such is as likely to mislead as to enlighten, for in this case neither novelist nor essay nor aesthetic fits very neatly within the usual boundaries of these terms.

Tanizaki's literary career spanned more than half a century—he lived from 1886 to 1965—and was as varied as it was long. Even the slender sampling of his novels available in English suggests something of the range of his imagination. *Some Prefer Nettles* (*Tade kuu mushi*, 1928–29) analyzes the conflicting emotions of a wealthy businessman as his unfaithful wife attempts to extricate herself from their marriage. *The Makioka Sisters* (*Sasameyuki*, 1943–48) is a minutely detailed portrait of four daughters of an old Osaka mercantile family, centering upon their attempt to find an acceptable husband for the beautiful but painfully reticent second sister, Yukiko. *The Key* (*Kagi*, 1956) portrays the sexual fantasies of an aging university professor who ultimately dies of the exquisite thrill of seducing his wife into an affair with a young lover. *Diary of a Mad Old Man* (*Fūten rōjin nikki*, 1961–62) is just that, the man's madness being a geriatric's consuming urge to satisfy his renewed sexual appetites before death overtakes him.

But the facet of Tanizaki's talent to which *In Praise of Shadows* belongs—his deep, even scholarly, interest in the traditional culture of Japan—may not be so readily apparent to the reader of the English translations. The scenes set in the puppet theatre in *Some Prefer Nettles* and the overtones of courtly sensibility that pervade *The Makioka Sisters* hint at this fascination; but its most direct manifestation was a body of historical fiction, only a small part of which has been translated. We have in English but two chapters of *The Mother of Captain Shigemoto* (*Shōshō Shigemoto no haha*, 1949–50), an eerie novel set in the ninth century, and a meager assortment of novellas and short stories, three of which are conveniently accessible in Howard Hibbett's *Seven Japanese Tales*—a mere fraction of the whole. And in addition to the historical fiction, Tanizaki spent a vast amount of time translating *The Tale of Genji* (*Genji monogatari*, ca. 1010) into modern Japanese; his rendition is as impressive for its historical and philological erudition as for the beauty of its language.

In *Praise of Shadows*, then, is the work of an extraordinarily learned novelist, and not simply a charming example of that flourishing genre, the literary man's essay on a nonliterary subject. The point is worth noting, for successful novelists in Japan are inundated with requests to hold forth on subjects that are often far removed from their knowledge; and their witty but airy ramblings on the latest political scandal, the housing problem, impressionist painting, or whatever, abound in the best newspapers and magazines. Tanizaki himself must have contributed several such pieces, as we surmise from his reference to being interviewed on the subject of unusual foods. But when he writes of traditional aesthetics, he speaks with authority of matters he cared about intensely. *In Praise of Shadows* is anything but the "empty dreams of a novelist."

"A well-stocked mind, perhaps," a critical reader might answer, "but a vagrant mind." And there is no denying that Tanizaki does wander—from architecture to toilets to jade to women to food—often with only the most tenuous of transitions, and quite as often turning back to repeat himself. To the Western reader trained to expect symmetry and logical progression in an essay, the urge to edit Tanizaki is at times almost irresistible. He has a perverse habit of shifting without warning from a tone of high seriousness to something near facetiousness; as when he recommends the toilet as a major source of poetic inspiration. His descriptions of lacquerware under candlelight and women in the darkness of the house of pleasure are perfect jewels; but would they not stand out to better advantage removed from the company of that murmuring bowl of soup and Einstein's trip to Kyoto? Yet to do so would drain the life of *In Praise of Shadows*, for Tanizaki's "essay" works in ways different from the Western essay, and demands the freedom of his seemingly haphazard style.

One of the oldest and most deeply ingrained of Japanese attitudes to literary style holds that too obvious a structure is contrivance, that too orderly an exposition falsifies the ruminations of the heart, that the truest representation of the searching mind is just to "follow the brush." Indeed it would not be far wrong to say that the narrative technique we call "stream of consciousness" has an ancient history in Japanese letters. It is not that Japanese writers have been ignorant of the powers of concision and articulation. Rather they have felt that certain subjects—the vicissitudes of the emotions, the fleeting perceptions of the mind—are best couched in a style that conveys something of the uncertainty of the mental process and not just its neatly packaged conclusions.

Thus it was that the compilers of the great classical anthologies, perhaps the most painstakingly structured compilations in the history of any literature, deliberately muted the sense of seasonal progression by frequent backtracking, and insisted upon a background of quite ordinary poems to set off the truly stellar compositions. And thus it is that Tanizaki's subject requires the shadowy style in which he treats it. Questions of the sort he raises have no final answers, and the mind of the writer who takes them up must always be groping, his statements always tentative. Susan Sontag has put the matter well in explaining her choice of style in "Notes on Camp": "To snare a sensibility in words, especially one that is alive and powerful, one must be tentative and nimble. The form of jottings, rather than an essay (with its claim to a linear, consecutive argument), seemed more appropriate for getting down something of this particular fugitive sensibility." Tanizaki would surely claim the same for the aesthetic he attempts to delineate.

Tanizaki's aesthetic speaks for itself and needs no explication, but it should be pointed out that his is not in every way an orthodox view of Japanese taste. For one thing, he conspicuously refrains from claims of some mysterious aesthetic sensibility in the Japanese genes. (We could forgive him if he did; the notion is centuries old and has the endorsement of the most eminent artists and scholars.) That the Japanese sensibility is in some ways unique is to be sure one of his main points, but he traces the uniqueness to more basic—and more believable—sources than "national character." Architecture developed as it did because of climatic conditions and the nature of available building materials. Gold served as a reflector of light as well as an ornament. "The quality that we call beauty . . . must always grow from the realities of life." And to Tanizaki this meant the whole of life, the base as well as the noble, eating and defecating as well as playgoing and the contemplation of calligraphy. Here lies another reason for following uncritically the erratic course of this essay. His descents to the earthy plane of toilets and recipes are as vital to his aesthetic as his ascents to the ethereal realm of ancient temples and the Nō. Few will follow him quite so uncritically as to agree that the traditional conception of female beauty was the inevitable result of having yellow skin; but we must admit that his insistence upon basic and natural causes contributes much to the eloquence of his argument.

The consequence of such an argument is an essentially pessimistic aesthetic, the aesthetic not of a celebrant but of a mourner. Tanizaki holds no hope for the survival of a sensibility that grew from a way of life now passing out of existence. By 1933, when *In Praise of Shadows* was written, much of what he described had either perished or was preserved, foooil likc, in sur-roundings that betrayed its true beauty. Traditional building materials and appliances were being replaced by glittering Western inventions. Gold-flecked lacquerware had been rendered garish by electric light. Floodlamps had turned the Kabuki into a "world of sham." Had he written later in his career he might well have added the Nō theatre and perhaps the Japanese house to his list of the moribund.

Here again Tanizaki runs counter to orthodoxy. His pessimism (and probably his earthiness too) would not be at all popular with the modern artistic establishment: the "masters" of flower arrangement, tea ceremony, calligraphy, painting, dance. Many of these people make handsome livings by their art, and, as the government's chosen cultural emissaries, have been influential shapers of the image of Japanese culture that is packaged for export. The implication that their art is stillborn could not but be resented. Tanizaki, however, would dismiss it as cold and sterile, too far removed from the sources of its life to claim any vitality. That scattered vestiges of excellence still survive he would not deny; and anyone who has seen for instance a votive performance of Nō on the weathered outdoor stage of a temple or shrine must agree that they do survive. But for Tanizaki a museum piece is no cause for rejoicing. An art must live as a part of our daily lives or we had better give it up. We can admire it for what it once was, and try to understand what made it so—as Tanizaki does in *In Praise of Shadows*—but to pretend that we can still participate in it is mere posturing.

Mrs. Tanizaki tells a story of when her late husband decided, as he frequently did, to build a new house. The architect arrived and announced with pride, "I've read your *In Praise of Shadows*, Mr. Tanizaki, and know exactly what you want." To which Tanizaki replied, "But no, I could never *live* in a house like that." There is perhaps as much resignation as humor in his answer.

In Praise of Shadows (In'ei raisan) was first published in the December 1933 and January 1934 issues of *Keizai ōrai*. In 1954 Edward G. Seidensticker published a selection of translated excerpts interspersed with commentary in Volume I, Number 1, of the *Japan Quarterly*. This article was later reprinted in the January 1955 issue of the *Atlantic Monthly*. The present volume is a complete translation of *In Praise of Shadows* which combines Professor Seidensticker's excerpts with my own rendition of the remainder of the essay.

Thomas J. Harper